“. . . for all have sinned and fall short of the glory of God,
and are justified freely by his grace through the redemption
that came by Christ Jesus.” (Injil, Romans 3:23-24)

How to read Bible references:

Matthew 24:35 = The Gospel of Matthew, chapter 24, verse 35

ISBN 978-1-908392-08-4

Serious Answers to Sincere Questions

Why did God command sacrifices?

Manzoor Masih

Dear Friend,

Asalaam O'laikum. You may wonder why I am writing you this letter. Usually when I write to someone I have never met, it is because I have something important to say. That's how I feel now.

Sacrifice is important to many people. For the Muslims Eid-ul-adha is a commemoration of a sacrifice. For Jews the Passover is a commemoration of a sacrifice. For Christians, Easter week is a commemoration of a sacrifice. Have you ever thought why sacrifices are so important in religious life? We know that God ordained sacrifice, because he told Abraham to sacrifice his son. He also commanded Moses to offer sacrifices. But why did God command sacrifices? This is an important question. Without the answer to this question we are left with total confusion about what God has been saying to mankind throughout all of history! It is important to examine the principles that God gave to Adam, Moses, Abraham, and Jesus as well as other prophets, so that we can learn more from about this very important matter.

Not long ago I met a well respected, intelligent Muslim professor of law who came into contact with a Christian man who loved and obeyed the Word of God. They had many good discussions. As time went on they discussed more and more about the differences and similarities of their beliefs. After some time, the Muslim professor decided to read more about the faith of his Christian friend. He found that there was one belief that was vitally important to his friend. It was the necessity of a sacrifice that would atone for sin. His Christian friend believed that without this, sinful man could not enter the presence of the One God who is absolutely holy. This man is to be commended for his diligent study and his important discovery. This is indeed a theme that runs clear through God's Holy Word and gives meaning to otherwise puzzling words and events.

May God bless you with his peace.

Dear Friend,

I ended the previous letter with a burning question, "Why did God command sacrifices?" I will begin to explain the answer in this letter.

When God made Adam and Eve, he put them in a perfect garden. But Adam and Eve disobeyed God's instructions so God had to expel them from the garden. At this time God told Adam and Eve the consequences of their actions, one of which was physical death. To the serpent, who tempted them, he said, " 'And I will put enmity between you and the woman and between your offspring and hers, he will crush your head and you will strike his heel.' " (Taurat, Genesis 3:15)

Here God promises that the power of Satan will be crushed through the seed of the woman. How will this happen? Has God given us further instructions concerning this? Yes, he has!

God begins to reveal the answer when Cain and Abel brought sacrifices to God. In the Taurat it says, "In the course of time Cain brought some of the fruits of the soil as an offering to the Lord. But Abel brought fat portions from some of the first-born of his flock. The Lord looked with favour on Abel and his offering, but on Cain and his offering he did not look with favour. So Cain was angry and his face was downcast. Then the Lord said to Cain, 'Why are you angry? Why is your face downcast? If you do right, will you not be accepted? But if you do not do what is right, sin is crouching at your door; it desires to have you, but you must master it.' " (Taurat, Genesis 4:3-7)

Why did God accept Abel's offering but not Cain's? In God's reply to Cain we find the answer to this question. God had obviously given clear instructions to Cain and Abel concerning what type of sacrifice needed to be offered. Abel brought the correct sacrifice which was an animal from the first-born of the flock. Cain did not bring the correct sacrifice. Cain brought a sacrifice of his own choosing instead of the sacrifice that pleased God. In the Bible it says, "There is a way that seems right to a man, but in the end it leads to death." (Anbia, Proverbs 14:12) "By faith Abel offered God a better sacrifice than Cain did. By faith he was commended as a righteous man, when God spoke of his offerings. And by faith he still speaks, even though he is dead." (Injil, Hebrews 11:4) A sober warning is also given to those who take the way of Cain. Because of his pride, he rejected God's authority and offered an unacceptable sacrifice.

We have learned that mankind has sinned against God and brought him shame by disobeying his commands. This sin must be paid for to satisfy God's righteous anger and uphold his justice and honour. God says, "The soul who sins is the one who will die." (Anbia, Ezekiel 18:4b) and "The wages of sin is death . . . ." (Injil, Romans 6:23)

Is sacrifice still required today? Does it still satisfy the righteous anger of God? Is there still a purpose in sacrifice? If so, what are the requirements for sacrifice, and what does it accomplish?

We will learn more about these matters in the following letters.

May God bless you with his peace,

Dear Friend,

We ended the last letter by asking a number of questions about sacrifice. In this letter we will learn how God provided a substitute, one life in the place of another. God, himself, has promised to help us understand these things. We should humble ourselves in prayer and ask him to teach us.

One day God told Abraham to go up into the mountain and to sacrifice his son. When they arrived at the place of sacrifice his son asked him where the sacrifice was. Abraham told him that God would supply the sacrifice. Then he bound Isaac and laid him on the altar. When he was ready to sacrifice him, the angel of the Lord called out to him and told him to stop. Abraham looked and saw a ram caught in the thicket. He took this ram and sacrificed it to the Lord. God had provided a substitute to take the place of the son that was to die. The ram died and the son lived. God sent a substitute to take the place of the condemned.

The story is told of a judge who had a very rebellious son. This son had caused his father much heartache and sadness. One day the son was brought to court for stealing. He was found guilty, and was brought before his father, the judge, for sentencing. The people in the courtroom knew of the special relationship between the judge and the thief. They waited with anticipation for the verdict. Would he forsake his duty as a judge, or would he uphold justice and punish him? As the crowd watched, the father pronounced the stiffest fine possible by law. The crowd was amazed, some almost angry, for they thought the father had been very hardhearted. Then to everyone's surprise, the father took off his judicial robes and stepping down from the platform said, "There is no way my son can pay this fine, but justice must be upheld. I will pay his fine for him."

As a result of Abraham's obedience and trust in God, God promised him, " '....through your offspring all nations on the earth will be blessed....'" (Taurat, Genesis 22:18) Who is this offspring who God promised would be a blessing to all nations?

Is it significant that God gave this promise at the same time that he provided a substitutionary sacrifice? I have come to believe it is. You may ask how I know. The answer is that God continues to reveal his plan in his Holy Word. We will see how God reveals his plan in the next letter.

May God bless you with his peace.

Dear Friend,

In the last letter we saw how God provided a substitute. Instead of Abraham's son being sacrificed, a ram was sacrificed. This is an important part in what God wants us to know about sacrifice. But did God only do this once in history? Did God allow for other substitutes? Again we pray that God would guide us in the straight way.

As we continue to read in the Holy Bible we come to the account of God delivering his people out of Egypt through his prophet Moses. (Taurat, Exodus 3 -15) God sent Moses to Pharaoh to ask him to let his people be set free from their slavery. Pharaoh would not let them go, so God sent plagues on the land of Egypt. The tenth plague was the worst, but God gave instructions to Moses how his people might be saved from this terrible plague. They were to take a year-old male without defect from the sheep or goats. It was to be kept from the tenth of the month till the fourteenth of the month. Then they were to slaughter it and eat the meat. The blood was to be applied to the top and sides of the doorposts of their houses. God explained the purpose for this, "On that same night I will pass through Egypt and strike down every first-born, both men and animals, and I will bring judgement on all the gods of Egypt. I am the Lord. The blood will be a sign for you on the houses where you are; and when I see the blood, I will pass over you. No destructive plague will touch you when I strike Egypt." (Taurat, Exodus 12:12-13) God did just as he said. There was no death among his people, but among the Egyptians every first-born died.

This is a good picture of another Lamb! Much later, the prophet John the Baptist (Yahyah) prophesied about a beloved Lamb that would take away the sins of the world. This sacrifice would be a perfect sacrifice, that had no defect. It would be a sacrifice that had been looked after for more than four days, a month, two months or even a year before the sacrifice. It would be the Lamb that had been prepared from all eternity. What better sacrifice could there be? Where could a more valuable sacrifice be found? By the blood of this sacrifice, many would be saved from death. God would provide a substitute, but not just a substitute. It would be a substitute that would conquer death and evil. God continued to explain about the sacrifices that were acceptable to himself.

May God bless you with his peace.

Dear Friend,

In the last letter we saw how God provided another substitute. The blood of this sacrifice was used to save many people from death. Again, we pray that God would guide us in the straight way.

God continued to fulfil his promise and explain how this first-born of the flock would be a substitute for human beings. Throughout history God revealed his character to man so that man could trust in the promises God gave. At the time of Moses, more than two thousand years had gone by, but God had not fulfilled his promises yet. He was still revealing his plan. To Moses he gave laws for his people to obey. But along with these laws he ordained sacrifices, for he knew the sinful heart of man. These sacrifices would further reveal his eternal purpose. He gave strict regulations concerning the sacrifices so that in the future people would recognize THE sacrifice he had promised who would crush the evil one.

Here are some of the regulations in the Taurat that God gave to Moses and his people. "For the life of a creature is in the blood, and I have given it to you to make atonement for yourselves on the altar; it is the blood that makes atonement for one's life." (Taurat, Leviticus 17:11) A BLOOD SACRIFICE WAS REQUIRED.

"If the offering is a burnt offering from the herd, he is to offer a male without defect ... it will be accepted on his behalf to make atonement for him." (Taurat, Leviticus 1:3a,4b) A PERFECT MALE WAS REQUIRED.

Since there was no perfect person to perform the sacrifice, the one that offered the sacrifices had to be covered by the blood of a perfect sacrifice as well. God gave instructions to Moses how to offer sacrifices. The sacrificer had to offer a sacrifice for his own sins and the sins of his household first and then he could come into the presence of God to offer a sacrifice for the sins of the people. (Taurat, Leviticus 16:2,3,6) THE SIN OF THE SACRIFICER NEEDED TO BE COVERED BY BLOOD.

God gave further instructions to Moses. He was to take two goats that were without defect and offer them to the Lord. One of the goats was sacrificed for the sins of the people. Then the sins of the people were confessed over the other goat and it was taken out and released in the desert to show that the sins of the people had been taken away. (Taurat, Leviticus 16:7a,8b,15a,21a,22) THE SINS OF THE PEOPLE WERE PUT ON ONE GOAT AND TAKEN AWAY, AND ANOTHER GOAT DIED FOR THE PEOPLE.

But this only covered sin for a while. Therefore these sacrifices had to be repeated year after year. (Injil, Hebrews 10:1-18) That is why the Injil says, "... it is impossible for the blood of bulls and goats to take away sins." (Injil, Hebrews 10:4) But it also says, "for all have sinned and fall short of the glory of God." (Injil, Romans 3:23) and "... the wages of sin is death (eternal separation from God) ..."(Injil, Romans 6:23)

So how can man know God and receive forgiveness of sin? God has revealed that every human being is guilty of sin, has shamed

God and deserves death. He has also revealed that the blood of animals will not take away sin. So, a perfect, sinless sacrifice is needed. Where can we get a sacrifice that is great enough, one that is sinless and one that can pay for the sins of the whole world? This leaves us with a dilemma or at least a question in our minds if we are honest. But the God who is above all and knows all things from the beginning, is never in a dilemma. God has revealed the answer to this problem. We will find out how in the next letter.

May God bless you with his peace.

Dear Friend,

This is the last letter, but hopefully it will not be the end of our searching out these matters.

In the previous letter we saw the requirements for a sacrifice that is acceptable to God but we were also left with a dilemma. Where will we get the perfect sacrifice that is so desperately needed to fulfil God's requirements and satisfy the righteous anger of God? And where will we find a sacrifice that is able to pay for all the sins of all peoples of the world?

The answer is in the Injil which God has faithfully preserved for us. In the Injil God tells us about the Lord Jesus Christ, the man in whom all the fullness of God lived. Being fully God and fully man, he is able to mediate between God and man and be the sacrifice that is needed. The following passages are from the Injil and speak of Jesus Christ. It says,"Christ has become a servant ... on behalf of God's truth, to confirm the promises made to the patriarchs so that the Gentiles may glorify God for his mercy ..." (Injil, Romans 15:8-9a) HE FULFILS THE PROMISES GIVEN TO ADAM AND ABRAHAM.

"Unlike other high priests, he does not need to offer sacrifices day after day, first for his own sins and then for the sins of the people. He sacrificed for sins once for all when he offered himself." (Injil, Hebrews 7:27) HE IS THE ONLY PERFECT SACRIFICE. HE IS THE ONLY PERFECT SACRIFICER.

"And so Jesus also suffered ... to make the people holy through his blood." (Injil, Hebrews 13:12) HE HAS OFFERED A BLOOD SACRIFICE FOR ALL MANKIND.

"For Christ died for sins once for all, the righteous for the unrighteous, to bring you to God." (Injil, 1 Peter 3:18) "... by one sacrifice he has made perfect forever those who are being made holy." (Injil, Hebrews 10:14) HIS SACRIFICE IS SUFFICIENT FOR ALL WHO COME TO GOD.

"Very rarely will anyone die for a righteous man, though for a good man someone might possibly dare to die. But God demonstrates his own love for us in this: While we were still sinners, Christ died for us. Since we have now been justified by his blood, how much more shall we be saved from God's wrath through him! (Injil, Romans 5:7-9)

Therefore, since we have been justified through faith, we have peace with God through our Lord Jesus Christ...." (Injil, Romans 5:1) HIS SACRIFICE BRINGS PEACE THROUGH FAITH IN HIS BLOOD.

Speaking of Jesus' eternal nature, the Injil says, "Now there have been many of those priests, since death prevented them from continuing in office; but because Jesus lives forever, he has a permanent priesthood. Therefore he is able to save completely those who come to God through him because he always lives to intercede for them." (Injil, Hebrews 7:23-25) HIS SACRIFICE CONTINUES TO BE EFFECTIVE.

Through his Holy Word, God shows us his love and faithfulness. The One True God is the God who has given us his promises and over thousands of years has faithfully fulfilled his promises to us. What we must not forget is that God has given his promises to you and me. In order to receive these promises, one must believe in the Lord Jesus Christ as the sacrifice for his sins. The sacrifice of Jesus is the only way for the righteous anger of God to be satisfied. The prophet, John the Baptist (Yahyah), prophesied this when he pointed at Jesus Christ, saying, "Look, the Lamb of God, who takes away the sin of the world!" It was Jesus who said, "I am the way, and the truth and the life. No one comes to the Father except through me." (Injil, John 14:6) Furthermore he says, "Come to me, all you who are weary and burdened, and I will give you rest. Take my yoke upon you and learn from me, for I am gently and humble in heart, and you will find rest for your souls." (Injil, Matthew 11:28-29)

Thank you for allowing me to share these thoughts from God's Holy Word with you! It is my desire that these letters may have answered many questions about what God has revealed to us in his Holy Word. These are only some of the teachings of the Holy Bible. The Holy Bible tells us much more about the character of God, how God works in the lives of people, teachings of the Lord Jesus Christ, miracles of the Lord Jesus Christ, and things that still are to come in the future. Most important, it explains fully how we can have peace with God. Because of these letters you may want to know more about the Holy Bible. I welcome any questions you have.

May God bless you with his peace.

Your friend,

Manzoor Masih.

If you would like to receive further information,
please contact us.

If you wish to make further study of the
Christian faith correspondence courses
in English, Arabic and French are available from:

Word of Hope Ministries, 22 New Street,
Rochdale, OL16 3PQ, United Kingdom

Email: **contact@word-of-hope.net**
Web: **www.word-of-hope.net**

Other booklets in this series:

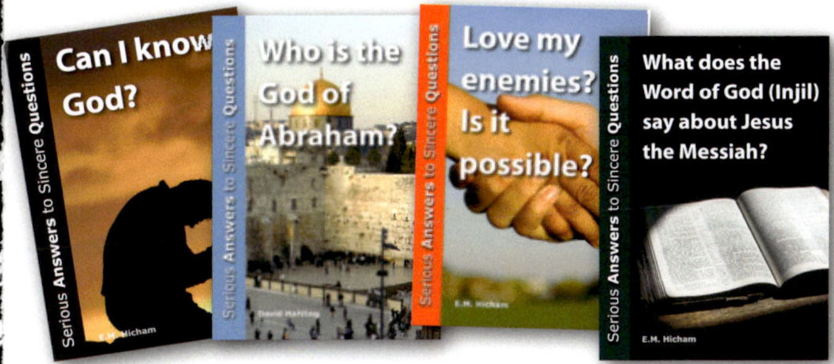

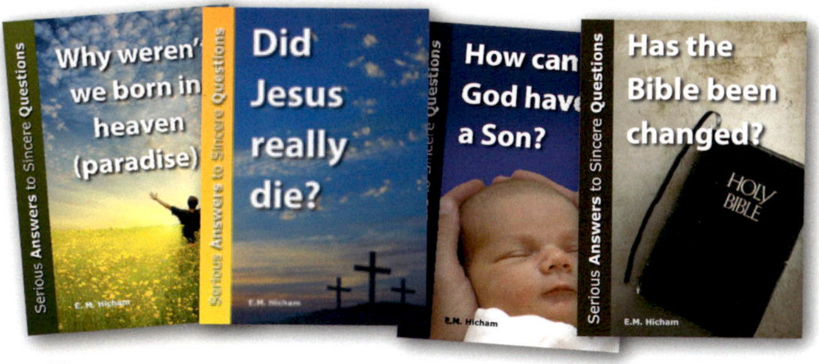

Also:

Scan to watch

11 minutes presentation of the gospel message.

Why did God command sacrifices?

Sacrifice is important to many people. For Muslims Eid-ul-adha is a commemoration of a sacrifice. For Christians, Easter week is a commemoration of a sacrifice. Have you ever thought why sacrifices are so important in religious life? We know that God ordained sacrifice, because he told Abraham to sacrifice his son. He also commanded Moses to offer sacrifices. But why did God command sacrifices? In this booklet the author answers this question through a series of personal letters he addresses to his Muslim friend.

Word of Hope Ministries

www.word-of-hope.net

9 781908 392084